SAY WHAT YOU SEE® f(
More Hugs. More respect.
Elegantly simple.

Readers' Comments

"I've been saying what I see with my children this week, and I am seeing some incredible changes already. I cannot believe all the hugs, kisses, and I love yous – and I have ENJOYED my children in an amazing way!"
— Jenn (children 2, 4) – Austin, TX

"So concise. There's more on each page of this little book than in all the other parenting books I've ever read."
— Teresa (child 5) – Waco, TX

"A simple, powerful way of working with children that's as applicable to the challenges of adolescents as it is to the challenges of infants." — John Snyder, Ele. Educator, Austin Montessori School, TX

"Say What You See makes what seems complicated, simple." — Risa Mandell, Clinical Social Worker – Philadelphia, PA

"I just had to buy two copies, one for myself and one to donate to our group's little library of sensational books. Thank you with all my heart for the book, I've already been putting it's lessons into practice with my 7 yr old and my new verbal actions are receiving positive responses from him." — Jane (child 7) – Brisbane, Australia

"'Say what you see' is a Magical Mantra!! I don't have to think about what the appropriate thing to say is, I just say what I see, and it works like magic :-)"
— Kavita (children 2, 6) – Austin, TX

"Very practical." — David (children 5, 10) – Ithaca, NY

"The Can Do response has COMPLETELY changed our lives...plus adding Strengths has helped our relationship. My son is so much happier; so am I...It's great!!"
— Rebecca (child 3) – Austin, TX

"Sandy presents the concepts and techniques in a simple, easy-to-retain way that every sleep-deprived, toddler-challenged parent will appreciate."
— Monica (child 2) – Attachmentmama.com

"I loved your book so much that I gave it to my Mom just after having read it. I'd love to pass one out to every teacher and parent that I know!"
— Milbrey (children 5, 9) – Austin, TX

"Say What You See is a great, easy way to relate to a child without getting stuck in 'What should I say?' What to say is right in front of you – you just need to put it into words objectively. I can always do that!"
— Beth (children 3, 7) – Ithaca, NY

"I'm part of several mom groups…When I mentioned the Language of Listening concepts to some of the moms, I think my passion and gratitude for what I've learned came across and the moms (especially the organizers of the groups) want to learn more. So that's why I bought five of the books!" — Kimberly (children 3, 4) – Austin, TX

"I was referred to your website by a relationships counselor... [I read it online and] can't wait to receive the booklet, I am donating the extra copies to my local kindergarten, child care centre and the primary school my children attend. Thank you for your inspirational work!"
— Lois (children 5, 6, 8) – Parkside, S. Australia

"This elegantly simple and wonderfully effective approach to parenting is THE essential tool for anyone desiring to help children grow to their highest potential! The more I read it, the more I appreciate the depth of love and wisdom that it embodies."
— Merrily Jones, MS, LPC – Austin, TX

"My best friend is the owner of a daycare. I told her about the part in the book where there was a problem with the child going to school...She tried it with her son who was having problems with starting kindergarten, and she was amazed at the results in something so simple. Just saying she understood."
— Angela – Elgin, TX

"No where else have I read or heard about such sane, compassionate, intuitive, and empowering strategies."
— Rev. Linda Martella-Whitsett – San Antonio, TX

"I swear by this book! This book makes it easy (and foolproof) to simply BE with others in whatever is going on for them – without taking it on yourself or becoming a "fixer." — Katherine Torrini, Creativity Coach – Austin, TX

"I'm taking the book to [a local family center]...I'm going to talk to all the therapists there and "testify!" to its value for parents. It's a terrific, easy to read-and-follow publication." — Dr. Susan Scott, LPC , Springs Therapy
– Colorado Springs, CO

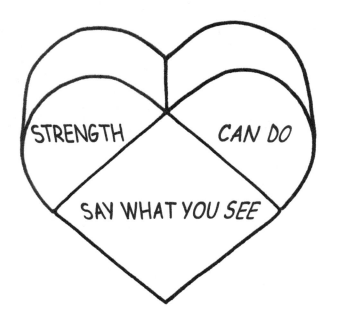

**The Language of Listening®
Heart Model**

Our three-part approach always starts with one thing:
First SAY WHAT YOU SEE to connect with children.
Add a STRENGTH when you see a behavior you like.
Add a CAN DO when you see a behavior you don't like.

It's that simple.

SAY WHAT YOU SEE®

for Parents and Teachers

**More hugs. More Respect.
Elegantly simple.**

Written and Illustrated by
Sandra R. Blackard

Some stories in this book are composites of actual events. Names are changed or details modified to protect the identities of individuals. Grammar intentionally reflects common usage.

4th Revised Edition

Published by Language of Listening 2012
Austin, Texas
www.languageoflistening.com

Language of Listening and SAY WHAT YOU SEE are registered trademarks of Sandra R. Blackard.

Cover design by Rita Toews
Photo by Patrick Blackard

ISBN-13: 978-0-9800015-2-5
ISBN-10: 0-9800015-2-8

The author and Language of Listening instructors are available for speaking engagements and private coaching. To contact us or to find more resources, products and services, visit our website:

www.languageoflistening.com

To the memory of my parents, Ruth and Harold Smith, who grounded me in love.

To Dr. Garry Landreth who opened my eyes to the child's world.

To my husband Pat and our daughters Colleen and Betsy who have given me a life I love.

To Eva Sim-Zabka whose vision and friendship have kept my dreams for Language of Listening alive.

SAY WHAT YOU SEE®
for Parents and Teachers

Contents

Acknowledgment

SAY WHAT YOU SEE simplifies, integrates and expands on communication techniques and concepts commonly used by play therapists as they were generously presented to me by a true hero for all children, Dr. Garry Landreth, as my mentor and in his books including, *Play Therapy: The Art of the Relationship*, Second Edition, (Brunner-Routledge 2002) and with Dr. Sue Bratton, *Child Parent Relationship Therapy (CPRT)*, (Routledge 2006).

In addition, I want to acknowledge Dr. Haim Ginott for his 1965 book, *Between Parent and Child*, and his media appearances that introduced a number of these groundbreaking concepts to the public. Although I had not read his work before initially writing this book, he significantly raised the level of parenting awareness in the world, ultimately making books like this one possible.

I would also like to acknowledge my family and friends for their years of enthusiastic support, and all the children in my life who have reminded me what it is like to be a child, especially my own two daughters, Colleen and Betsy, and my niece, Kylee.

<u>Please note</u>: Throughout the text, direct quotes from Dr. Landreth are indicated by a superscript L ([L]).

♥   ♥   ♥

PART I:

A New Perspective

-1-

A Valuable Experience

I'd been warned. Brandon was seven years old, always in trouble, and full of excuses. I was the parent volunteer assigned to be his buddy on the first-grade field trip to the zoo. I have to admit that I was uneasy about the assignment and would have preferred to accompany my own child that day, but I agreed.

After a frantic morning of child-herding as Brandon tried to run ahead to get to the next cage first, slip around the corner to peek behind the "Staff Only" door, and duck under the railing to get a closer look at the lion, the two of us sat down with the teacher and the other kids for a picnic lunch.

We had just finished eating when I looked up and saw Brandon grinning and aiming the straw in his juice box directly at me. Before I knew it, he squeezed the box and red punch flew onto my white t-shirt.

My usual reaction to reckless behavior after an exhausting morning would've been an angry, "Look at what you just did!" Indeed, the teacher had just such a look. But instead, I saw Brandon's look of horrified shock and responded to what I saw. I heard myself say to the teacher in a surprisingly calm voice, "It's OK! He didn't mean to do it." Then I said to Brandon, "You thought the box was empty!"

Upon hearing this, Brandon's tense shoulders relaxed, his little face shifted to remorse, and he nodded profusely. Instead of excuses, Brandon delivered a heartfelt apology. I got the sense that it was the first time in a long time that he had been understood rather than blamed for an accident.

The buddy assignment turned out to be valuable for us both. Each time he saw me for the rest of the school year, I got a big hug; I could tell he felt good about himself when he was around me. With one response, I'd demonstrated love and respect and was getting the same in return.

♥   ♥   ♥

Chapter 1 Notes

A Valuable Experience

♥ **When we demonstrate love and respect, that's what we get back.**

-*2*-

Responding to the Good in Children

When you were a child you might have heard the statement, "Do as I say, not as I do." Children instinctively know this doesn't work; adults wish it did.

The truth is that children <u>do as we do</u> far more naturally than they do as we say, especially when the two are in conflict.

Love and respect are the two things that matter most in our relationships with children. Like with Brandon, when what we "do" is show love and respect, that's what we get back.

Love and respect are easy to show to children who are behaving appropriately; but showing love and respect is challenging when children are behaving in ways we don't like. The trick to maintaining a loving and respectful relationship with our children is seeing the good in them regardless of their behavior. This requires a new level of understanding.

We gain a new level of understanding when we recognize that all behaviors are driven by healthy needs. By changing our focus from the behavior to the need it demonstrates, we can begin to see the good in children in all circumstances.

For example, children giving you hugs are demonstrating a need for human contact; so are children who tackle you from the side. If we react to aggression as though

 children are mean or reckless, we are likely to react with angry reprimands. If we recognize the need for contact, we are more likely to show children appropriate ways to get what they need — like a high-five or secret handshake to replace

the tackle. Understanding allows us to respond with love and respect rather than anger.

What about behaviors that are obviously bad like cheating? Even in cheating, understanding the need helps us focus on the good. The need demonstrated by cheating is the need to feel like a winner — a capable person who can achieve personal goals. This need is universally understood as good and healthy.

Children know that to feel like winners, they must experience winning. If winning doesn't come easily, children's innate drive toward health will automatically propel them toward winning in another form. For example, if children feel overwhelmed by the game of chess, they may switch to checkers. If they cannot win at checkers, they will avoid the game, only play against younger children, or cheat to win in order to prove to themselves and others they are winners.

Wanting to win is a good thing. When we focus on the drive to win rather than on cheating, we can understand the behavior and take actions that show love and respect. These might include allowing children to set the challenge level of games played with us by asking, "Do you want me to play hard or easy?"[L]; building self-confidence by placing children in activities in which they naturally excel; and teaching new skills when children are ready to advance.

When children are given appropriate opportunities for winning and mastery, they are able to regain their sense

[L] Direct quote from Dr. Landreth.

of capability without cheating. Children who see themselves as winners don't need to cheat; they have nothing to prove.

While we would like to focus on the good in children at all times, it is difficult to overcome our automatic reactions to "bad" behaviors. What stops us is our past, which is always with us in the form of judgment of others and ourselves. Probably by the time we were age seven, we had already decided that "good behavior=good person" and "bad behavior=bad person." ← No good there; why look?

These childhood judgments about good and bad are real to us. They were locked in place with a lot of emotion as "hot buttons" that occasionally block our ability to see our children objectively and respond with love and respect. For example, if we react with anger when children interrupt us, we are reacting to the judgment "interrupting is 'rude' or 'bad.'" Although formed in the past, this childhood judgment now blocks our ability to see the good in children who interrupt. An angry response is likely to follow.

If while reading this, you find yourself asking, "What is the good in children who interrupt?" you are ready to move beyond judgment and respond with objective observations; you are ready to say what you see.

When you say what you see, you remain in the present and are able to focus on the good in children. In the case of interrupting, judgments like "rude" are replaced with observations like, "You have something to say that you are excited about." Hearing this observation come out of your mouth will help you understand what the child needs and come up with an appropriate alternative like, "You can tell me in a minute," or for younger children, "Grab that thought and keep it in your pocket for a little bit longer, and then when I'm done, you can let it all out."

As parents and teachers, we want to be role models for seeing the good in other people. Seeing the good helps us keep children feeling good about who they are and about each other. There's no better way for children to experience love and respect. Love and respect are automatic when you say what you see.

♥   ♥   ♥

Chapter 2 Notes

Responding to the Good in Children

- ♥ **All behaviors are driven by healthy needs.**

- ♥ **Recognizing the need allows us to see the good in children regardless of the behavior.**

- ♥ **To allow children to set the challenge level of games ask, "Do you want me to play hard or easy?"[L]**

- ♥ **Love and respect are automatic when you say what you see.**

L Direct quote from Dr. Landreth.

-3-

Listening to Understand

Saying what you see creates a special kind of listening — listening with the intention of understanding. Listening to understand keeps us focused on the child instead of our past. It helps us see the good in children so children can see it in themselves.

How we listen determines how much children will share with us. Listening to understand puts them at ease. It helps children express themselves freely, feel good about themselves, and most of all, feel important.

To understand children, we must understand their points of view. As we all know, children see the world differently than adults. Everything children DO and SAY is a communication from their world to ours. From what they do and say, we can understand what they THINK and FEEL. Children love to be understood; even children who want to be a mystery feel connected when you say, "You're just a mystery to me!"

The desire to be understood is so great that it is actually a need. Children <u>must</u> continue to communicate until they feel understood. This is evident in the familiar repetition of "Mom, Mom! Dad, Dad! Teacher, Teacher!" or the common impulse of young children to tell about a pet rather than answer the question they were asked when called on in class.

Like their verbal counterparts, children who are "acting out" a communication tend to escalate their actions until understood. For example, if a child starts whimpering when dropped off at preschool, a parent saying, "But you like it here. Remember how much fun you had last time?" is not likely to work. When it seems that the parent doesn't understand, the child's only recourse is to cry harder or scream to communicate the severity of the problem.

If the parent were to say instead, "You really don't want me to go! You will miss me and feel very sad," the child would know his point was made — no further acting out required. If the parent were to look into the child's eyes before leaving and add, "I will be back at the end of school to pick you up," the child would sense the parent's confidence in his ability to handle separation and cope with sadness. Soon he would be able to calm himself and focus on the activities of the class. By returning promptly after school, the parent would be building trust, thus making future drop-offs easier for the child.

With an upset child, understanding works like a fire extinguisher. I've seen a wailing five-year-old with a handful of crumpled papers cry harder when teachers and other children tried to comfort

her by saying, "Don't cry. Those book marks you made were nice!" This same child was able to begin calming herself down the instant she heard the words: "Those didn't turn out the way you wanted. You feel frustrated!" accompanied by a mood-matching, frustrated stomp of the adult's foot.

Similarly, a child fussing on a long plane ride was able to relax into the ride after an adult made a sympathetic childlike pout and said, "Long plane rides are just awful!" Understanding produces instant results.

♥   ♥   ♥

Chapter 3 Notes

<u>Listening to Understand</u>

♥ **Listening to understand puts children at ease.**

♥ **Everything children DO and SAY is a communication.**

♥ **Children must contintue to communicate until they feel understood.**

♥ **With an upset child, understanding works like a fire extinguisher.**
Example:
> "That didn't turn out the way you wanted. You feel frustrated!"

PART II:

How to SAY WHAT YOU SEE

_-4-_

Demonstrating Understanding

Body language is an important part of saying what you see. Along with your words, your actions and facial expressions must match the child's mood. Use your arms, hands and face to express intense emotion, or keep a calm, quiet demeanor to match concentration. Body language helps us demonstrate understanding to children.

Body language includes getting down to the child's level. Be aware that to a child, an adult looking down over crossed arms feels like judgment. Seat yourself next to the child at a table or desk, kneel on bended knee, or sit on the floor with the child when possible. Watch intently to understand; remember "eyes equal ears to a child."[L]

L Direct quote from Dr. Landreth.

When you are down at the child's level, you can begin to SAY WHAT YOU SEE. Your objective observations will incorporate what you see, hear, and otherwise sense. Saying what you see is the basic building block of understanding. It's the one thing that can change a bad moment with a child into a rewarding one.

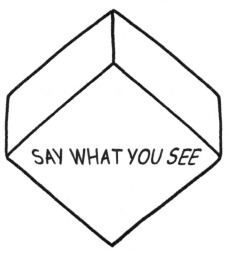

The best part, for those of us who may be concerned about saying the right thing, is that saying what we see takes the pressure off of us. What to say always comes directly from the child. We are there simply to hear the child's perspective and let the child know that we heard.

While listening, do not give answers or try to teach; instead you are there to learn from the child about the child. If needed, teaching can come later, <u>after</u> you show that the child's point of view is understood. If a child is not listening, you need to listen to the child first. Children cannot listen until they are heard.

To put a child at ease and provide the kind of listening that is needed, set your intentions on observing without directing. Simply follow the child's lead. Allow children to decide how near to you to stand, and let them direct the conversation or activity. Children need to feel safe to communicate.

Simon says, "Take one baby step closer."

Make observations using statements, not questions. Sometimes we use questions to appear polite or to avoid being wrong and mistake this for keeping the child in the lead. A great thing about children is that when you say what you see, children know you are listening to understand, and they make sure you do. If something matters to them, they won't let you get it wrong.

Statements encourage communication and help us follow the child's lead. Questions can feel threatening and inhibit a child's expression, as though there is a "right" answer.

Questions such as, "What's in your hand?" or "Why are you holding that rock?" tend to cause a quick hand-behind-the-back response. Whereas, the non-threatening statement, "You've got a rock," encourages a flow of information like, "It's MY rock. I found it with my Grandpa when we went for a walk in the woods. My dog was there; his name is Chips. My mommy doesn't like dogs..."

Questions also carry assumptions. Even something as innocent as, "What do you want to do next?" reveals our pervasive adult perspective by assuming the child has a plan.

Alternatively, saying what we see keeps us present and open to the child's perspective as in, "Looks like you're done with that." Free from external pressure to make a decision, the child can say, "Yep!" and begin to look around for something else to do or just relax for a minute and stare out the window.

Questions can also be directive. Questions like, "Don't you think scissors would work better for cutting out that circle?" direct the child to do something the adult way rather than encourage creativity.

Instead, when you say what you see as in, "You're tearing the paper around that circle," the child can tell you, "I like the way the edges look. They make my circle look like the sun," or the child can say, "This isn't working. I need scissors." Either way, the child's opinions and problem solving skills are encouraged.

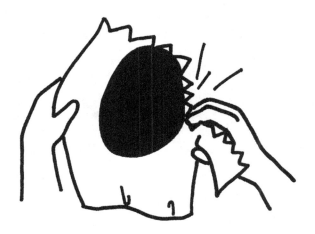

The final type of counterproductive question is the non-question. We usually use this one when we are annoyed and far from seeing the good in the child. Non-questions are basically a way to deliver criticism or introduce a lecture as in, "What are you doing in there?" Appropriately, non-questions result in defensive non-answers like, "Nothing!"

To put children at ease and get real information, back-up and simply say what you see as in, "I hear banging noises in there." You might actually get an answer like, "I just accidentally knocked some books off the shelf," or a self-correction like, "Sorry. I'll be more careful next time."

Most questions distance us from children. We see something, our thought processes automatically tack on our perspectives and opinions, and a question pops out. When we add this extra layer of adult mental processing, the result is a disconnection with the child. To reconnect, even after a question has popped out, back-up and state the observation that gave rise to the question — simply say what you saw. Kids always allow do-overs.

♥   ♥   ♥

Chapter 4 Notes

<u>Demonstrating Understanding</u>

- ♥ **"Eyes equal ears to a child."[L]**

- ♥ **Children cannot listen until they are heard.**

- ♥ **To demonstrate understanding, SAY WHAT YOU SEE.**

- ♥ **Follow the child's lead.**

- ♥ **Match the child's mood with your words, actions, and facial expressions.**

- ♥ **Use statements instead of questions to make observations.**
  Example:
    "You've got a rock."

L Direct quote from Dr. Landreth.

-5-

SAYing WHAT YOU SEE

SAY WHAT YOU SEE applies directly to what the child is DOING, SAYING, FEELING, and THINKING:

DOING
When you say what you see the child doing, focus on the process, not the product. Adults tend to think the point of working with craft materials or building blocks is to create a specific thing. Children may simply enjoy the experience of the moment.

Saying what we see helps us stay in the moment with the child. It returns us to the experience of making marks on crisp, white paper or handling soft, cool play dough and allows the children we watch to create more freely. With crayons, statements like, "You are drawing blue, back and forth across the top of the paper, coloring really fast," and "You're working carefully to color in that shape, covering all the little white spaces that are showing through," or with clay, "You pressed really hard right there and made a hole," and "You're squishing the clay between your fingers," demonstrate that we are paying close attention to what matters to the child at the moment. Understanding builds deep connections.

The connection is especially clear with younger children who will often test you playfully to see what they can get you to say. For example after hearing the observation, "You  poked your finger into that play dough," the child might look up expectantly and poke it again, just to see if you will respond. You'll know it's a game if when you say, "You poked it again!" the child breaks into a giggle and pokes it yet again. As long as you are willing to play the poking-looking-giggling game, it will continue. Spontaneous, child-led games like these are a great way to connect with young children.

For older children who already focus on the product, you may identify finished objects as needed to let them know you understand their intentions. At the same time, be sure to point out the mental and physical processes of the moment.

For example, "You're making a house. Seems like you know what you're doing. You're adding a door right

there. Looks like you're concentrating on making the lines very straight. And there's the door handle. Now you're adding brightly colored curtains to the windows; now a garden with three kinds of flowers; and there (point), a bird flying overhead. You decided to add lots of details to get it just the way you wanted!" Saying what you see helps children appreciate their efforts and abilities and increases their self-confidence.

SAYING

Saying what you see the child saying is done in two ways: repeating exactly what the child says or rephrasing it. In either case, be sure to use the same important words or phrases the child uses. Words often have special meanings to children; using their own words says you understand.

For example, if a child runs to you excitedly and says that a big fire truck just zoomed by, repeat by saying enthusiastically, "A <u>big</u> fire truck just <u>zoomed</u> by!" or rephrase by saying, "It was <u>big</u>, and it <u>zoomed</u>!" This

will draw a quick nod from the child and possibly more information like, "I want to be a fireman when I grow up!"

The shorter your response, the better. All children will confirm with body or voice when you are right. They can't help it. Watching for physical responses and noticing when your comments open the door for further communication will keep you on track. Don't worry about missing a word or phrase that matters to children. When children know you are interested, they will repeat it for you.

FEELING

When you say what you see the child feeling, the most important thing to remember is to accept all feelings, even those you don't like. Saying what you see celebrates emotions like joy and pride and validates other emotions like sadness and anger. It also helps us contain our need to make everything all better, which in turn strengthens our children's abilities to solve their own problems or handle disappointments.

Using a tone that matches the child's mood, simply say what you see the child feeling, taking clues from the child's demeanor and what the child does and says. For example, "You feel proud of the way you drew that!" or "You're feeling sad about losing your

dog. You wish it would come back," or "You just squashed that snowman flat! You feel angry when you can't make the play dough do what you want." (Notice the part about how nice the snowman was is missing?)

Say what you see to let a child know you understand and to send the message, "It is OK to feel what you feel. You can handle these emotions. You will be able to calm yourself when you are ready."

Remember first that the expression of feelings is a communication, and second, that children must continue to communicate until they are understood. Saying what you see tells them you understand. If children choose inappropriate methods to express their feelings like hitting people or breaking things, you can add a CAN DO as presented later in this book to help them find an appropriate outlet.

A third point to remember is that children are always right about how they feel. Extreme emotional reactions that seem out of line are never about the problem at hand. The level of the reaction isn't wrong; the source is.

For example, if a child has a meltdown reaction to a sibling taking a toy, it's not about the toy. It's more likely to be about a series of unresolved toy snatchings and the consequent feeling of having no control over life in general. While loss of one toy may not warrant a meltdown, feeling helpless in life does. It's a very scary feeling!

Regardless of the source of the upset, to help a child accept extreme feelings and calm down, say what you see in a tone that matches the desperate feelings of the moment. Adding the observation, "You calmed yourself!" when the child has completely recovered will help the child recognize self-control, which is the first step toward regaining a sense of control over life.

Children are also always right about what they like and don't like, and what they want and don't want. In fact, the child is the only one who really knows. So rather than telling a protesting child, "Of course you like bananas. You just ate one yesterday," and suffering the escalating proof of the child spitting out the food or even gagging, try validating the dislike by saying what the child feels as in, "You don't want it. You don't even like it, and here it is, part of your lunch!"

The child's first response might be agreement, "Yea, and I'm not eating it!" But, if you continue saying what you see with, "You're not eating it! No way," in a few minutes you just might hear, "Well, maybe I'll just take one bite..." as the child proceeds to eat the whole thing. With no need to defend or prove a dislike, kids sometimes change their minds. Validation allows kids to experiment with likes and dislikes until permanent tastes are formed.

Once formed, personal likes and dislikes should be respected and honored whenever possible. When this is not possible, as in school drop-offs, medicine, or shots, validate the child's upset by saying what the child feels as in, "You really don't like getting shots. You remember they hurt. You wish you never had to have any." The more the child feels understood, the easier the experience will be for everyone involved.

THINKING
Saying what you see the child thinking allows you to check your understanding of a child's perspective. Again, taking clues from the child's demeanor and what the child does and says, say what the child appears to be thinking. These statements are about the child's thoughts and intentions, not yours. They help confirm that you understand.

"Looks like," "sounds like," and "seems like" can be used to introduce these observations. For example, "Looks like you want to go to the park," or "Sounds like you don't want to be here," or "Seems like you want me to do something," invite clarification. When children feel at ease rather than interrogated, they will often provide whatever information is needed to help you understand.

♥   ♥   ♥

Chapter 5 Notes

SAYing WHAT YOU SEE

- ♥ **To respond to <u>doing</u>, focus on the process, not the product.**
  Example:
  "You are drawing blue, back and forth across the top of the paper, coloring really fast!"

- ♥ **To respond to <u>saying</u>, repeat or rephrase using the child's important words and phrases.**
  Examples:
  "A <u>big</u> fire truck just <u>zoomed</u> by!"
  "It was <u>big</u>, and it <u>zoomed</u>!"

- ♥ **To respond to <u>feeling</u>, validate all feelings, even those you don't like.**
  Example:
  "You're feeling sad about losing your dog. You wish it would come back."

- ♥ **To respond to <u>thinking</u>, say what the child appears to be thinking.**
  Start with:
  "Looks like..." "Sounds like..." "Seems like..."

-6-

Adding STRENGTHs

For children to see their strong points, we must see them first. Centering responses point out children's inner strengths. They are responses that strengthen a child's sense of self and build self-confidence. Centering responses are all about the child.

Centering reduces dependence on outside approval, which reduces the negative effects of peer pressure later in a child's life. If we raise children to live for our approval, we are inadvertently setting them up for difficulties in their pre-teen and teen years.

Middle school and high school years are the years when children begin to build their own community of peers with whom they will navigate the rest of their lives. Peer approval naturally replaces previously established adult approval in their lives and will have the same degree of influence on their decisions.

Teaching children how to say no will not work if their sense of self depends on outside approval. Our use of centering responses helps children grow up looking inward rather than to others to decide what's right for them.

To help children become centered and look inward, use objective acknowledgment rather than praise whenever possible. Children act according to who they believe they are, just as we do. If I believe I am a parent or teacher, I will work to become a good role model for children; if I believe I am an artist, I will draw; if children believe they are good learners, they will pursue a college degree; if children believe they are considerate, they will become aware of other's feelings, etc. Acknowledgment affirms who the child is.

Our beliefs about who we are come most often from our successes and failures — those of which we are aware. By watching for and acknowledging children's successes, we can make children aware of their inner strengths, so they can define themselves accordingly.

Acknowledgment has far greater impact on a child's idea of self than praise. Praise is about what <u>we</u> think and what <u>we</u> like; acknowledgment is about <u>the child</u>. Acknowledgment builds confidence because it says who the child is, not just what we think.

Children accept praise only if they already agree. If children have a different opinion of themselves, praise can break trust. For example, if we praise children for being smart or attractive and they don't already believe they are, they may either think we're just being nice and won't be able to trust us to tell them the truth, or they will think we don't understand them. In both cases, their belief that to be accepted they have to be something they are not will be confirmed, and feelings of pressure and resentment or giving up will result. For building self-confidence and connecting with children, acknowledgment is the best choice.

To acknowledge a child objectively, SAY WHAT YOU SEE and add a STRENGTH:

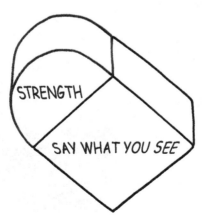

By adding a strength after saying what you see, you tie your comment to an immediate, objective observation and provide the child with proof instead of your opinion. Saying for example, "You read the textbook and figured out how to solve the math problem yourself. That shows you are a <u>good learner</u>," makes the child's intelligence undeniable.

All children have every possible inner strength; they just don't know it. When you want a child to see a particular strength, watch for it in everything the child does.

Start with the basic building block by saying what you see, then name the strength to prove to a child it's there. For example, "You finished making that even though

you seemed frustrated at times. That shows you are determined," or "You told me right away that you spilled the milk. That shows you are responsible." (See page 69 for a partial list of strengths. Blank space is included, so you can keep adding to the list.)

Acknowledgment helps teenagers see their strengths, too. To help teenagers recognize their ability to dress appropriately, for example, you need to see it first. This can be hard, especially if you don't like a teen's clothing choices. But if the clothes are accepted somewhere like the teen's school, you can say, "You know I don't like the way you dress, but you seem to choose clothes that are allowed by the school. That tells me you know how to dress appropriately for the situation." Teenagers who believe they can dress appropriately will have an easier time choosing a suit for an interview or a modest outfit for a funeral than those who believe they can't.

Sometimes you might not realize you saw an example of a strength until later. No matter; kids allow do-overs. You can go back at any time, say what you saw, and name the strength then. Though some may pretend not to, children of all ages love it when they hear that they've gotten your attention, even when they were not with you. Similarly, if you hear yourself use praise, follow it immediately with an acknowledgment of what you saw and add the strength it shows. The evidence presented in the acknowledgment will validate the praise.

Additional centering comments to use when you say what you see include:

"You did that just the way you wanted to!"[L]
"It's what you think that matters!"[L]
"You stopped yourself!"[L]

Picture children growing up with powerful thoughts like these to guide them. Teens and pre-teens who believe their opinions matter and believe they have self-control look inward rather than to peers for approval.

L Direct quote from Dr. Landreth.

Chapter 6 Notes

Adding STRENGTHs

- ♥ **For children to see their strengths, we must see them first.**

- ♥ **Acknowledgement builds confidence because it says who the child is, not just what we think.**

- ♥ **To acknowledge a child, SAY WHAT YOU SEE and add a STRENGTH.**
  Example:
  > "You told me right away that you spilled the milk. That shows you are <u>responsible</u>."

- ♥ **Centering responses point out children's strengths.**
  Examples:
  > "You did that just the way you wanted to!"[L]
  > "It's what you think that matters."[L]
  > "You stopped yourself!"[L]

[L] Direct quote from Dr. Landreth.

-7-

Adding CAN DOs

Defining boundaries for children's behavior is often the biggest challenge for parents and teachers. None of us wants to be mean or be the bad guy stopping kids from getting what they want or need. What we want is for children to learn to control themselves, so we can enjoy their company as we raise them and teach them.

Children need rules. Rules create boundaries that provide children with the opportunity to experience self-control. By bumping into boundaries, children learn they have the ability to stop themselves. Rules are centering because they allow children to master self-control.

Kids seem to know this instinctively. Watch a child walk down a sidewalk; how long before the child makes up a rule about not stepping on cracks? Or at any time, "Last one there is a rotten egg!" Kids call their rules games; we, on the other hand, tend to call our rules mean.

To shift this kind of thinking, consider walls: although they don't appear the slightest bit mean, walls are boundaries. Walls block children's access to rooms. Children can't walk through walls, but they usually don't get upset about it — walls just <u>are</u>. Effective rules are like walls.

We want the rules we make for children to be objective statements of what is. The way we state a rule and how consistently we apply it establish its nature as a wall. When subjective or inconsistent, our rules are like doors. Doors sometimes open and sometimes don't. While children may cry and beat on a door to make it open, they don't often spend time beating on a wall. Children accept walls.

The first step for making rules is clarifying your own boundaries. Beyond the standard rules you make for your child's safety, you need to determine what boundaries to set for your own sanity. If you have been taught to put others' wishes first, defining boundaries to maintain personal comfort is hard. But, isn't that what you want for your children?

If you are not sure where to begin, start with noticing what is OK with you and what isn't. While a child banging a toy against your couch cushion might not be hurting anything, if it doesn't feel right to you, you can say, "I don't like that. I don't know why, I just don't like it," and find something that the child <u>can do</u> like bang the toy against a bedroom pillow. If you have time, a pillow fight would be even better and completely take the child's focus off of the couch.

For children to respect their own likes and dislikes and stay out of compromising situations, you need to give yourself permission to make rules that reflect your personal boundaries. For example, I don't like loud noises, so I have rules for the noise levels in my house and my car — screaming is for outdoors.

Role-modeling acceptance of your personal boundaries equals role-modeling self-respect. Your children will do as you do.

In making rules, to help determine if you should allow a behavior, ask yourself, "Can I consistently allow this?" On the other hand, to avoid over-restricting children's behavior, ask yourself, "Is this rule needed?"

When you make a rule, omit the reasons. Explaining why to gain children's cooperation often backfires. Reasons create an opening for debate and manipulation. If you say, "Balls are not for throwing in the house <u>because you might break something</u>," you can expect children to defend their throwing skills with words, "But I won't break anything!" or with actions like throwing the ball lower next time rather than stopping. When in doubt, remember the wall analogy: walls aren't for walking through — no need to say why.

When children question your rules with, "Why?" consider responding, "If you really want to know, I'll be happy to explain, but if you want me to change my mind, it's not going to happen." The directness of the response brings honesty and openness to the moment.

If the child actually wants to know why, you can state your reason. If the child then begins to argue, simply say what you see and restate your position, "You think I might change my mind, and I'm not going to." Remember to observe the child's reaction and say what you see as needed until the child feels heard as in, "You are angry with me. You don't like my rules. You wish you could make your own rules."

To increase cooperation, acknowledge every movement the child makes toward following a rule. For instance, after you've ruled out ball throwing in the house, if the child throws the ball again in a more controlled way, acknowledge the cooperation and restate the rule, "You threw the ball lower this time. Balls are still not for throwing inside. They are for outside." Children find it easier to cooperate when their good intentions are recognized.

If you find you cannot be consistent with a rule, check to see if your reason might actually be the boundary. For example, if the more controlled throw works for you, breaking things is actually your boundary, not throwing in the house. To win cooperation, acknowledge the child for being right and adjust the rule saying, "You found a way to throw the ball that won't break anything — lower and away from the lamp. You can throw the ball inside that way."

Wrongly interpreting attempted cooperation as rebellion or rigidly applying rules children know aren't right, leaves children feeling unappreciated and misunderstood. Over time, repeated misunderstandings will cause children to lose respect for authority. You may know teens who will no longer listen or are sure their parents and teachers don't know anything. In contrast, repeated understanding and recognition of children's attempts to cooperate build respect that carries through the teen years.

Once you have established a rule, to gain a child's cooperation, simply SAY WHAT YOU SEE and add what the child CAN DO:

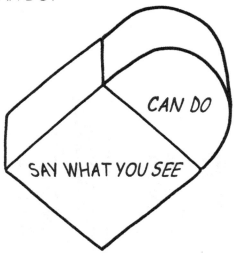

When a child is drawing on the wall, the CAN DO sequence sounds like this: "Looks like you want to draw. You <u>can</u> draw on this paper." In most cases, the rule is clear and does not even need to be stated.

Start with the basic building block by saying what you see. This helps you remain calm and gives you time to think. Focusing on what the child can do shifts your thinking to the positive: What is an appropriate way for the child to meet the need or the want? If you can't think of a way try, "Hmm. There must be something you can do," and turn the problem solving over to the child. When children recognize that you are on their side, they stop themselves from crossing boundaries, cooperate willingly, and come up with amazingly creative solutions.

If a rule needs to be clarified, particularly for younger children, state the rule using a no-fault, common sense statement like, "The wall is not for drawing on," and

return your focus to what the child can do as in, "You can tape several papers together and put them up on the wall to draw on," or "You can use your chalk and draw on the fence." Use your creativity and your child's to select an appropriate CAN DO that meets the need.

If the need can't be met here and now, the CAN DO can be a different time like "after dinner" or "next time" or a different place like "outside" or "at home." By fulfilling on your promise of later or elsewhere, you build trust; by focusing on what the child can do, you encourage creativity and affirm, "Where there's a will there's way."

To help children wait, explore what they want in wishes. For example, "I know you're hot and hungry and want ice cream right now! You wish you could have a great big cone, or a whole room full, or an ice cream mountain! You wish you could slide down through all that cold ice cream!" It's easier for kids to wait when someone understands how they feel.

Saying what the child can do also avoids the pitfalls of taboos. Taboos are guaranteed to challenge kids and focus their interest on the problem.

Rather than forbidding things like spitting or saying potty words, offer an alternative place, "Sounds like you learned a new word today that you want to say. You can

say it in the bathroom." After a few minutes of giggling while shouting it into the mirror, the fascination of the word will wear off. If it comes up again just say, "Sounds like you're not done yet. You can go back in the bathroom and say it until you get it all out!"

Avoid taboos; gain cooperation!

The complete CAN DO sequence for the ball throwing situation mentioned above and a few others sounds like:

"Looks like you want to throw the ball. (The ball is not for throwing inside.) You can throw it outside."

"You are very frustrated and want to tear something! (The book is not for tearing.) You can tear yesterday's newspaper."

"You are so angry you want to hit something. (I am not for hitting.) You can pretend the pillow is me and hit it as hard as you want!"

"You really want that toy! (The toy is not for taking from the store without paying.) You can save up your allowance, and in two weeks you can buy it."

If you hear yourself say, "OK?" after stating a rule as in, "The wall's not for drawing on, OK?" check to see what you are really asking. Unless you are willing to change the rule when the child says, "No!" this is a non-question that you will want to avoid. Clearly you don't need the child's permission to define a boundary. However, if your meaning is, "Do you understand the rule?" then say, "Understand?" instead of "OK?"

The CAN DO sequence is flexible. Try only saying what you see when the appropriate behavior is understood.

The fewer words the better. Instead of saying, "Your dirty clothes are on the floor. The floor is not for clothes, the laundry basket is," simply point and say "dirty clothes." Likewise for brushing teeth try "teeth," or for washing hands try "hands." In class when children know the rules for quiet time, cleaning up, and pushing chairs up to the table try saying only "talking," "messy floor," or "chairs." Single word reminders encourage children to think and solve problems on their own.

Similarly, when the child's goals and the rules are understood, feel free to jump straight to what the child can do as in, "You can run <u>outside</u>," "You can have dessert <u>after you eat your dinner</u>," or "You can practice pouring <u>in the bathtub</u>." The CAN DO helps children cooperate.

♥   ♥   ♥

Chapter 7 Notes

Adding CAN DOs

♥ **Effective rules are like walls.**

♥ **Acknowledge every movement the child makes toward following a rule.**

♥ **To encourage self-control and creativity, SAY WHAT YOU SEE and add what the child CAN DO.**
Example:
> "Looks like you want to throw the ball. You can throw it outside." OR "There must be somewhere you can throw it."

♥ **Avoid taboos; gain cooperation.**
Example:
> "You can say potty words in the bathroom."

♥ **Single word reminders encourage children to think and solve problems on their own.**
Examples:
> "Teeth." "Hands." "Talking."

PART III:

Conclusion

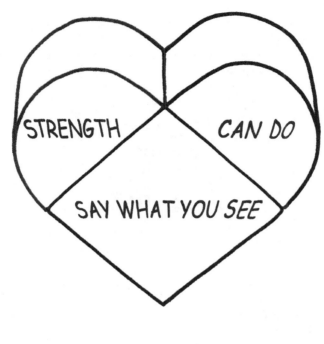

-*8*-

Changing the Future

When you put the three parts of the Language of Listening together, you have a brilliantly simple way to respond to any situation with love and respect.

SAY WHAT YOU SEE using neutral observations to connect, validate, and calm upsets. When you see a behavior you like, add a STRENGTH to help children become centered and self-confident. When you see a behavior you don't like, add a CAN DO to gain cooperation and encourage creativity. Using the three parts together during the formative years allows children to grow up in touch with their natural strengths knowing anything is possible.

In the case of a two year old who doesn't get what she wants, feels angry, and tries to hit you, using all three parts together can sound like this:

SAY WHAT YOU SEE:
"You wanted to go outside, and we have to stay in. You're so angry, you feel like hitting!"
CAN DO:
"You can hit the bop bag (or the pillow, mattress, etc.)!"

SAY WHAT YOU SEE:
> "Look at you hitting that! Now you're kicking it!
> You feel powerful when you jump and kick like that.
> Look at you go!"

As the child regains her sense of personal power, she will
be able to calm herself down and address the original
problem. The more you remember to point out her
strengths, the quicker she will be able to draw on them
this time and the next time she gets upset. It can sound
like this:

STRENGTH:
> "You found a way to get all that anger out and calm
> yourself right down! That shows self-control!"

CAN DO:
> "There must be something you can do inside..."

You can explore some options with her if needed, but
chances are good that if she has fully regained her sense
of personal power, she'll come up with something to do
inside on her own. Kids are resourceful by nature; and,
of course, when she demonstrates her resourcefulness,
you'll be there to name the strength!

But don't forget the best part. If you fall into an old
pattern of questions, anger, blame, etc. as all of us do
from time to time, you can always go back. The do-over
can be in the next moment, the next day, or the next
week. As long as you go back sometime, your child will
get the benefit of being heard and understood. The only
way to do it incorrectly is to not do it at all.

The more comfortable you get with the three parts of the Language of Listening, the more you will hear it coming back from the children around you. So don't be too surprised when you hear your child say, "I did that just the way I wanted," instead of getting frustrated; or "I went upstairs by myself and turned on my own light. I'm brave," without looking to you for praise; or "This play dough lid is stuck. I can try pulling harder," without running to you for help.

My personal favorite was when I heard my teen say, "Mom, you look angry. Something didn't go the way you wanted it to," rather than assuming my upset was about her. The ability to listen to other people's points of view without taking it personally comes easily for kids raised with the Language of Listening.

Now, if saying what you see is new to you, you will want to start slowly. Focus on the basic building block first — SAY WHAT YOU SEE. It's the key to improving any interaction with a child.

For an easy start, watch a child at play and practice saying what you see for no apparent reason as in, "You've got the zoo toys," or with school work try something like, "Looks like you're ready to do your math problems."

At first you might get a puzzled look as the child awaits the usual questions, but when none follow, notice the results: sometimes more conversation, sometimes greater focus on the task at hand. But regardless of the results, pat yourself on the back and say what you see to yourself, "You remembered to say what you see!" Do that a few times, and you'll be amazed at how quickly you master this basic listening skill.

Once you are comfortable saying what you see, adding STRENGTHs and CAN DOs will follow naturally. Hearing  yourself say, "You came home when you said you would," will lead you straight into a STRENGTH like "responsible." Likewise, an objective observation like, "You are pouring water on the floor," will naturally call for a CAN DO like, "You can pour that in the kitchen sink."

Imagine how different the future will be when all of our children are raised and taught by adults who say what they see. Then think how easy it will be for them to pass these skills on to their children, and you will get a glimmer of the impact we can have on the future here and now.

Because kids naturally do what we do, all we have to do is remember one thing, SAY WHAT YOU SEE, and together we can change the world in one generation.

♥   ♥   ♥

Chapter 8 Notes

<u>Changing the Future</u>

- ♥ **SAY WHAT YOU SEE** using neutral observations; when you see a behavior you like, add a **STRENGTH**; when you see a behavior you don't like, add a **CAN DO.**

- ♥ **Get comfortable by practicing the basic building block first — SAY WHAT YOU SEE.**

- ♥ **STRENGTHs and CAN DOs will follow naturally.**

PART IV:

Supplementary Material

<u>List of Strengths</u>*

DOING WORDS: capable, careful, considerate, cooperative, danger-spotter, dependable, fair, friendly, fun, generous, gentle, goal oriented, helpful, kind, masterful, motivated, observant, organized, patient, paying attention, persistent, problem solver, punctual, reliable, resourceful, responsible, self-controlled, self-directed, strive for excellence, team player, tidy, unstoppable

SAYING WORDS: assertive, direct, honest, polite, respectful, tactful

FEELING WORDS: affectionate, balanced, bold, brave, caring, compassionate, confident, courageous, easy going, empathic, energetic, enthusiastic, forgiving, inspiring, intuitive, joyful, loving, loyal, optimistic, peaceful, powerful, sensitive, spirited, supportive, tolerant

THINKING WORDS: appreciative, aware, clever, contemplative, creative, curious, decisive, determined, good learner, idealistic, insightful, intelligent, know what you like, know what you need, know what you want, planner, smart, thoughtful, understanding

*<u>Please note</u>: This is only a partial list. Add new words or adjust groups as needed.

Recommended Reading
(Available at www.languageoflistening.com)

Cline, Foster and Fay, Jim. *Parenting with Love and Logic.* (Pinion Press 2006)

Cline and Fay. *Parenting with Love and Logic for Teens.* (Pinion Press 2006)

Cohen, Lawrence. *Playful Parenting.* (Ballantine 2002)

Faber, Adele and Mazlish, Elaine. *How to Talk so Kids Will Listen, and Listen so Kids Will Talk.* (Collins 1999)

Faber and Mazlish. *Siblings Without Rivalry.* (Collins 2004)

Faber and Mazlish. *How to Talk so Kids Can Learn.* (Scribner 1996)

Ginott, Haim. *Between Parent and Child.* (Three Rivers Press 2003)

Goertz, Donna Bryant. *Children Who Are Not Yet Peaceful: Preventing Exclusion in the Early Elementary Classroom.* (Frog 2001)

Kellam, Theresa. *The Parent Survival Guide: From Chaos to Harmony in Ten Weeks or Less.* (Routledge 2009)

Language of Listening®

Premises

1. **SWYS:** Everything children <u>do</u> and say is a communication. Children must continue to communicate until they are heard.

2. **STRENGTH:** All children have <u>every</u> possible inner strength. Children act according to who they believe they are.

3. **CAN DO:** All behaviors are driven by <u>healthy</u> needs. Children need 3 things: experience, connection, power.

4. **OVERALL:** All growth is through <u>acceptance</u>. Children set exactly the right level of challenge for growth.

My Notes

1. Share this book with my friends!

2. Pat myself on the back for saying what I see!

3. Make notes of my say what you see Aha!s and successes:

My Notes

<u>My Notes</u>

About the Author

Award winning author and parenting expert, Sandra R. Blackard, created the Language of Listening parenting approach outlined in this book, and founded the Language of Listening company for parenting and personal growth. Sandy's down-to-earth perspective helps adults see the world through the child's eyes, making sense of what children say and do.

After receiving a master's degree in art conservation, Sandy worked at the Kimbell Art Museum in Fort Worth, Texas, restoring paintings. The hours spent pouring over a microscope determining what was original and what was not honed her skills of scientific observation, which became the cornerstone of her future work in parenting and personal growth.

While working at the museum, she met and married Patrick, a lighting director and videographer. Later she became an independent collection preservation consultant, so she could work from home and raise their two daughters, Colleen and Betsy.

Faced with the challenges of parenting two children eighteen months apart, she sought the assistance of a world renowned play therapist who became her mentor, Dr. Garry Landreth, Founding Director of the Center for Play Therapy, University of North Texas, Denton. The principles of play therapy he presented transformed her understanding of children so radically that her overriding thought was, "Why doesn't every parent know this?!!" She spent the next twenty years dedicated to that mission.

Through relentlessly sharing and refining what she had learned — like how to help previously clinging Colleen skip off to Kindergarten without a backward glance, and help three-year old Betsy go brush her teeth without crossed arms or a defiant, "No!" — the Language of Listening was born. It's a unique blend of proven parenting skills, play therapy principles, and scientific observation distilled down into a simple three-part approach that always starts with saying what you see and ends with finding strengths regardless of the behavior.

Along the way, Sandy developed an instructor's manual for her classes that later served as a model for *Child Parent Relationship Therapy (CPRT) Treatment Manual* (Routledge 2006) which she co-authored with Drs. Landreth, Bratton, and Kellam. *SAY WHAT YOU SEE for Parents and Teachers* is referenced as a parent resource in the *CPRT Treatment Manual* and quoted in Dr. Kellam's subsequent book, *The Parent Survival Guide: From Chaos to Harmony in Ten Weeks or Less* (Routledge 2009). In 2012, *SAY WHAT YOU SEE for Parents and Teachers* was named a NAPPA Gold Winner (National Parenting Publications Awards).

Sandy and her family now call Austin, Texas, their home. She frequently leads Language of Listening classes at Austin Montessori School and is available for private coaching and speaking engagements. To learn more about Language of Listening or to contact the author, go to:

www.languageoflistening.com

♥   ♥   ♥

PREVIEW

Peek inside
the next book...

The Three Basic Needs

Changing Challenging Moments
into Rewarding Ones

Susie won't share her toy with her sister. Jenny aims a log at a friend. Billy dumps water on an unsuspecting girl. Kids of all ages complain. Where's the good in that?

<u>Look for the Need</u>
The easiest way to find the good in children, regardless of their behavior, is to look for the need. To make it simple, you can look for three basic needs:

- EXPERIENCE — I've got this body, now what can I do with it?
- CONNECTION — I need to feel noticed, understood, validated, and loved.
- POWER — I need to feel confident, in control of myself, and able to make an impact on my world.

While a lot more can be said about these three basic needs, the important thing to know right now is that whatever the child is already doing is meeting one or more of these needs. The goal of the behavior reveals the need. When you look for the need behind the behavior, you find the good. Here's how it works:

Susie's Toy
When I was visiting a neighbor, her two young daughters, three-year old Natalie and four-year old Susie, were playing in another room. After a while my neighbor went to check on them. When I heard raised voices, I joined them to see what was happening. I saw Susie protectively carrying a small box of toys towards the closet and Natalie crying angrily after her, "I wasn't done yet!" The older child hid the box quickly and stood guard saying defensively to her mother, "But she's not old enough to play with these toys!" Her mother said she needed to share her toys and tried to point out that Natalie was three now and a big girl. Susie's retort, "Three's not a big number, only four is!" made it clear that arguing about age would not solve the problem.

This was a fight over sharing. Susie appeared "bad" and was backed into a corner trying to justify her selfish behavior. At least that's how it might seem. The choices in dealing with a "selfish child" are limited: a) make the older child share her toys against her will, b) deny the younger child the toys, or c) take the toys away. None of these choices would have helped Susie share willingly. However, intentionally looking for the need brought different choices into focus. Since her goal was to control her possessions, or at least some of them, the primary need in this case was power.

The mother graciously allowed me to intercede. I said one simple thing to Susie that changed everything. I offered a can do: "I bet there are things in this room that you can share with your sister." She looked stunned at first, then her face brightened. She ran and got a book saying, "I can share this book!" As she handed it to her sister, I acknowledged her by saying what I saw, "You found a book to share!" Next thing we knew she was standing by her sister holding out a toy from the coveted box saying, "I can share this with her, too."

This was the ideal outcome, Susie sharing willingly and Natalie feeling valued. By granting Susie control of which possessions to share, her need for power was filled, and her natural generosity was allowed to shine through.

Jenny's Throw
Five-year old Jenny was playing in my back yard with a friend. They were running, chasing and having a great time. The next time I looked up, I was shocked. Jenny was laughing while holding a log over her head with both hands, ready to throw it at her buddy.

Before I learned to look for the good, I would've seen a "bad kid" with a gleeful intent to injure and would have yelled angrily then taken her aside for a lecture. Instead, I saw a child who simply needed information to meet

her need for connection, and I called out, "Stop! That will hurt him!" She stopped cold, dropped the log and came up with her own can do for connecting safely with her friend — off they ran for a fun game of tag.

In talking about it later, I found out that Jenny thought it would be funny, like in the cartoons. My assumption that she wanted to connect with her friend was right. The lesson about throwing was learned without a lecture, and Jenny came away knowing she cares about her friends.

Billy's Water

One summer day I was watching a two-year old boy play with a bucket in a public wading pool. He carefully filled his bucket, looked around, and spotted an 18-month old girl sitting in the water. He ran over to her and with a big grin dumped the water on her head. She sat there with a surprised look on her face, not sure how to react until both mothers swooped in. The little girl, seeing her mother's concern, began to cry. The other mother yelled, "Billy, that was mean! You go tell her you are sorry!"

Billy's face fell. He suddenly became a "bad kid" and the little girl became a victim.

Rather than seeing a "bad kid," what could Billy's mom have seen if she were looking for the need? Some teens answered this way: "Maybe he wanted to share his bucket of water or just wanted to see what she would do." If the mom had seen it as a desire for connection or a learning experience instead of an attack, she could've said what she saw and taught him the first rule of play as a can do, "Looks like you want to play. You can ask first."

Imagine the difference this would've made in Billy's and the little girl's senses of self. Billy would have gained social confidence, and the girl would've felt like what she wants matters.

Complaints to Wishes
An instant way to find the good in children's complaints or frustrations, is to listen for what they wish or want. Wishes and wants are direct expressions of healthy needs.

Responding to a young child's complaint of, "I'm so bored," with the typical fix of, "You have plenty of toys. Go play with them," will create more resistance, since the child now has to prove his point. However, stating the wish, "You wish you had something fun to do," can either shift the child into action right then, if the need is experience, or give him the chance to tell you more, which might actually be something like, "I wanted to play with Johnny today, and he can't play." That's an entirely different need (connection), and one that playing with toys alone won't fill. Scheduling a play date for another

time could make a big difference in how the rest of the day goes and even make the other non-Johnny options more appealing to him.

This works for any age because our wishes and wants also point us toward our strengths. For example, you can respond to a grown child's frustration of, "Nothing I do is good enough," with "You want it to be, and it's frustrating when every-thing you try seems to fall short." Saying what you see and stating the want can elevate her from a complainer to a person who wants to do things well. It also makes you a safe person for her to confide in — exactly what she needs in order to move from generalized complaints, which are too overwhelming to handle, into specifics that she can do something about.

What You Look for You Will Find
When you remember that all children have every possible inner strength, it becomes clear that what we see in our children is determined not by what is there, but by what we look for. If you try to look for the good, but react with a negative judgment instead, just remember, that you are

reacting to a behavior, not a need. It's what you have been trained to do your whole life, so give yourself a break, and try again.

In your do-over, start by saying what you see. Saying what you see actually changes what you see and helps you look for the three basic needs. For example, saying, "You're wiggling in your chair," helps you see that the child wants to move and helps you recognize the need for a physical or sensory experience; "You're whining. You wish I would help you put on your shoes," the need for connection; "You're screaming at me. You want me to do something," the need for connection and power.

Saying what you see and stating the wish or the want help you recognize your child's needs. This instantly moves you away from automatic negative reactions toward can do's and strengths. When faced with a challenging behavior, say what you see to find your child's wants or wishes and look for the three basic needs. It's the quickest way to find the good.

♥   ♥   ♥

End preview.

You can find out more about the three basic needs and the Language of Listening in the articles and resources on our website.

✂

Cut here to post the heart model on your refridgerator.

✂

Language of Listening®

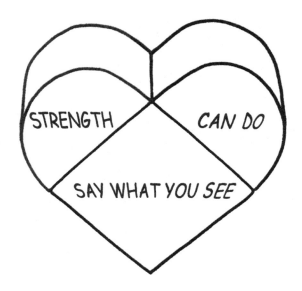

Premises

1. **SWYS:** Everything children <u>do</u> and say is a communication. Children must continue to communicate until they are heard.

2. **STRENGTH:** All children have <u>every</u> possible inner strength. Children act according to who they believe they are.

3. **CAN DO:** All behaviors are driven by <u>healthy</u> needs. Children need 3 things: experience, connection, power.

4. **OVERALL:** All growth is through <u>acceptance</u>. Children set exactly the right level of challenge for growth.

Made in the USA
Coppell, TX
27 October 2020